About This Book

Title: *The Sun*

Step: 1

Word Count: 88

Skills in Focus: All short vowels

Tricky Words: a, of, sky, Earth, rock, the

Ideas For Using This Book

Before Reading:
- **Comprehension:** Look at the title and cover image together. Ask readers what they know about the sun. What new things do they think they might learn in this book?
- **Accuracy:** Practice saying the tricky words listed on page 1.
- **Phonemic Awareness:** Have readers point to the word *sun* in the title. Practice taking apart and putting together the sounds. Ask readers to count the sounds in the word by tapping a new finger to their thumb for each new sound they hear. Ask: How many sounds are in the word *sun*? What is the first sound? Middle sound? Ending sound? Change the /s/ to a /f/. What word is it now? Repeat with the word *run*. What other *-un* words do readers know?

During Reading:
- Have readers point under each word as they read it.
- **Decoding:** If readers are stuck on a word, help them say each sound and blend the sounds together smoothly. Be sure to point out any short vowel sounds.
- **Comprehension:** Invite students to talk about what new things they are learning about the sun while reading. What are they learning that they didn't know before?

After Reading:
Discuss the book. Some ideas for questions:
- Where is the sun? When can we see the sun?
- What does the sun do?

The Sun

Text by Laura Stickney

Reading Consultant
Deborah MacPhee, PhD
Professor, School of Teaching and Learning
Illinois State University

PICTURE WINDOW BOOKS
a capstone imprint

The sun sits up in the sky.

It is hot.

Earth is a big rock.

But the sun is not.

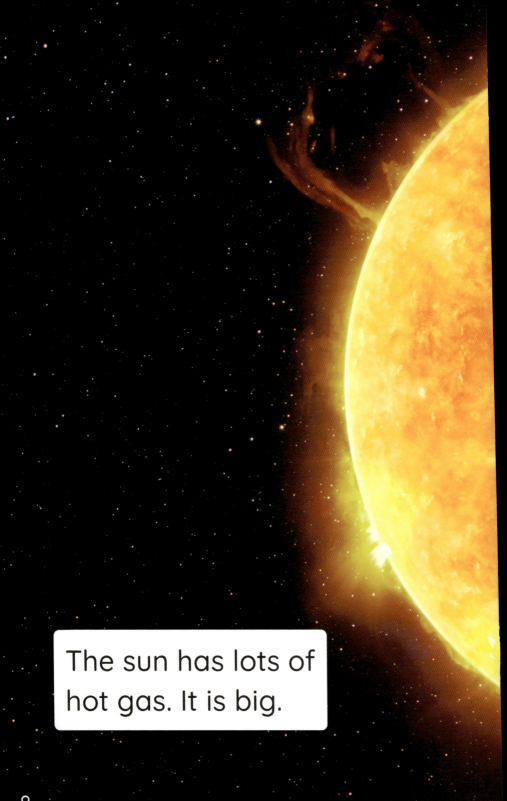

The sun has lots of hot gas. It is big.

The sun is up.
Earth is lit up.

Cats get up.

Dogs get up.

The sun gets Earth hot.

The sun can get us hot.

Put on sun hats.
Sit in the sun.

The sun has set. It is not up.

Earth is not lit up.

More Ideas:

Phonemic Awareness Activity

Practicing Short Vowels:
Tell readers they will segment the sounds of story words containing short vowels. Say a short-vowel story word for the readers to practice segmenting the sounds. Tell the readers to make a movement such as hopping in place or clapping their hands as they break apart the word, with one movement for each sound they say. Begin with *can*. They will hop once for /c/, again for /a/, and once more for /n/. Ask: What sound was first? What was the middle sound? Ending sound?

Suggested words:
- sun
- hot
- can
- rock
- big

Extended Learning Activity

Let's Draw!
This books talks about the sun. Ask readers to draw a sun on a piece of paper. Have them draw the rays of the sun. Alongside each ray, ask readers to write down a word or phrase describing the sun.

Published by Picture Window Books, an imprint of Capstone
1710 Roe Crest Drive, North Mankato, Minnesota 56003
capstonepub.com

Copyright © 2026 by Capstone.
All rights reserved. No part of this publication may be reproduced in whole or in part, or stored in a retrieval system, or transmitted in any form or by any means, electronic, mechanical, photocopying, recording, or otherwise, without written permission of the publisher.

Library of Congress Cataloging-in-Publication Data is available on the Library of Congress website.

ISBN: 9798875226922 (hardback)
ISBN: 9798875228988 (paperback)
ISBN: 9798875228964 (eBook PDF)

Image Credits: iStock: DONOT6, 22-23, mycola, cover, SStajic, 4, valio84sl, 24, egal, 6-7, Yuliya Taba, 1, 18; Shutterstock: Africa Studio, 19, aleks333, 5, Anna Hoychuk, 12, ANURAK PONGPATIMET, 16-17, Ed Connor, 2-3, Harry Beugelink, 14-15, Jukka Risikko, 20-21, Lukasz Pawel Szczepanski, 8-9, Simon Bratt, 10-11, Yarrrrrbright, 13

Printed and bound in China. 6274